DISCOVER SERIES
SCIENCE

CIENCIA

Átomo

Atom

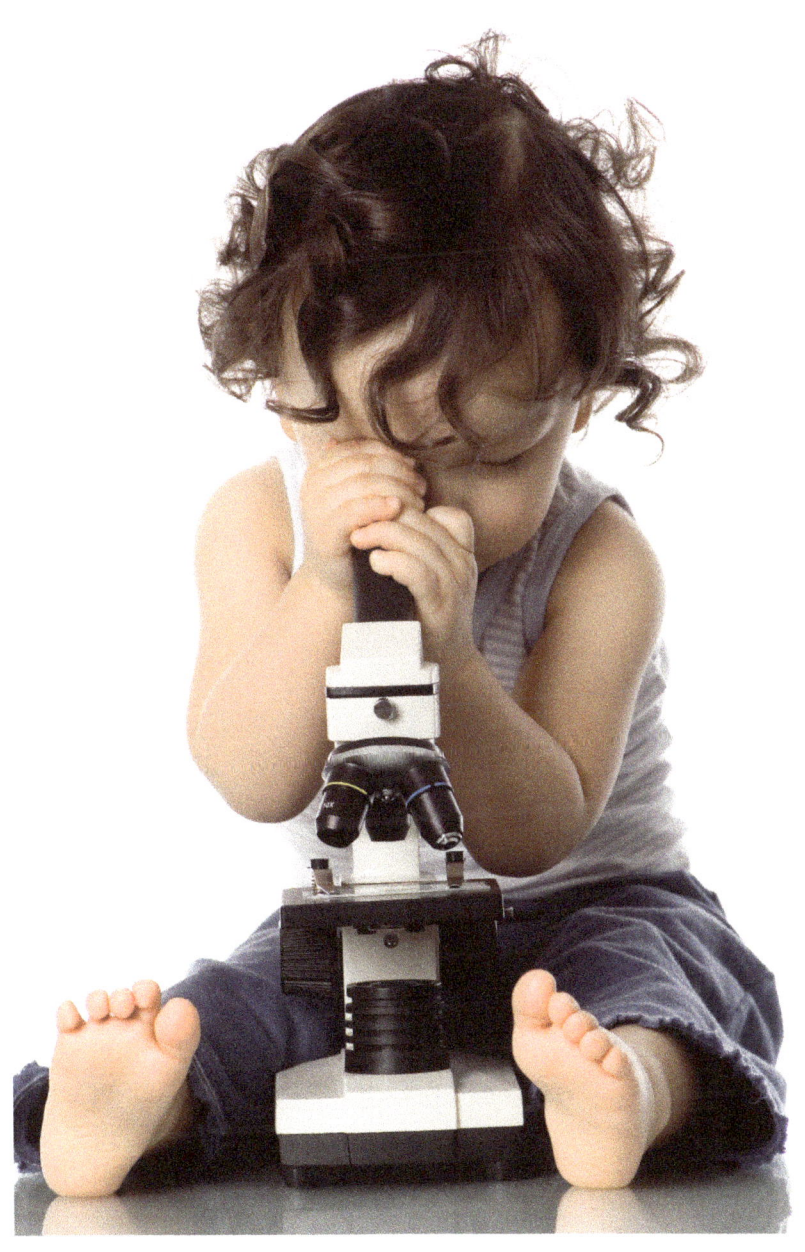

Viales de sangre

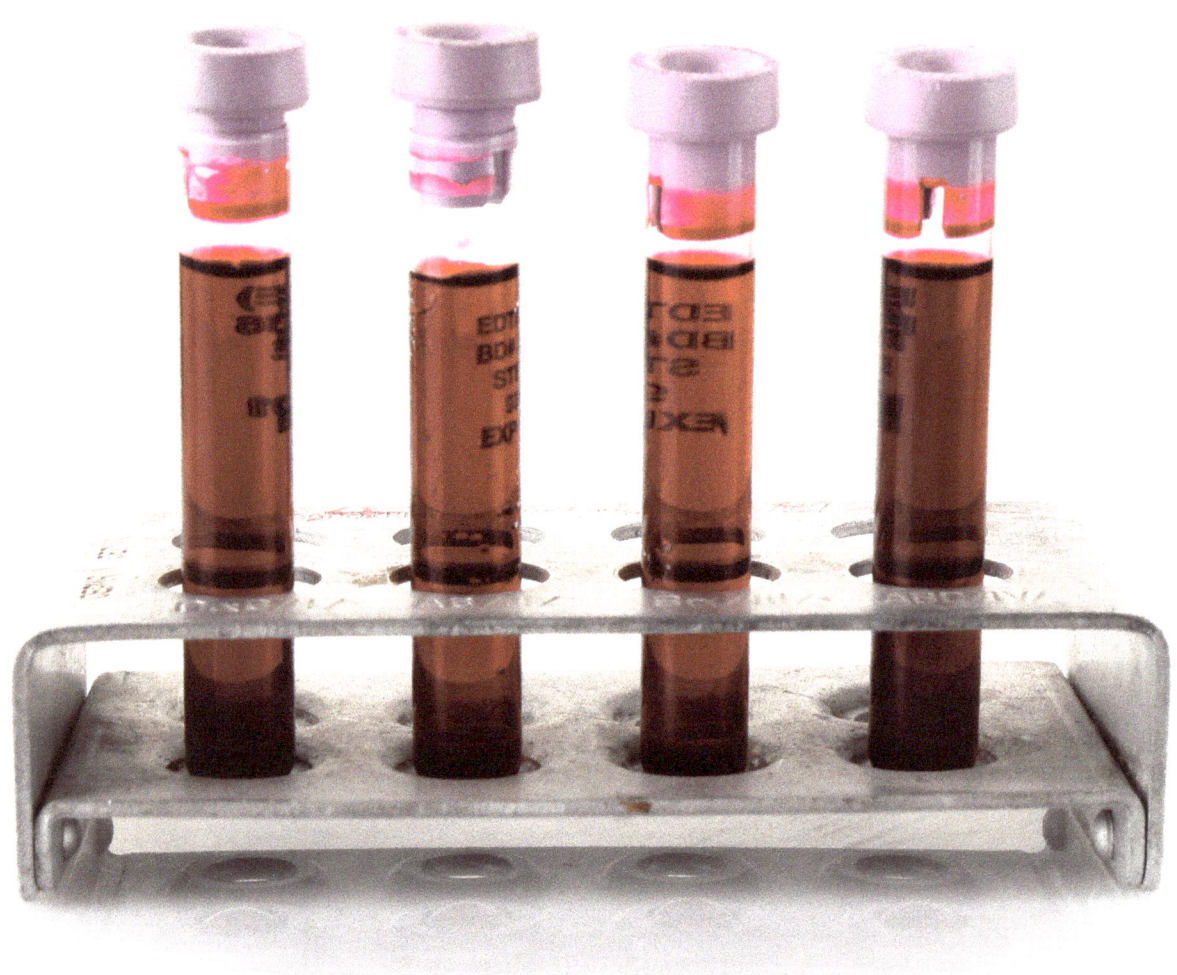

Blood Vials

Mechero Bunsen

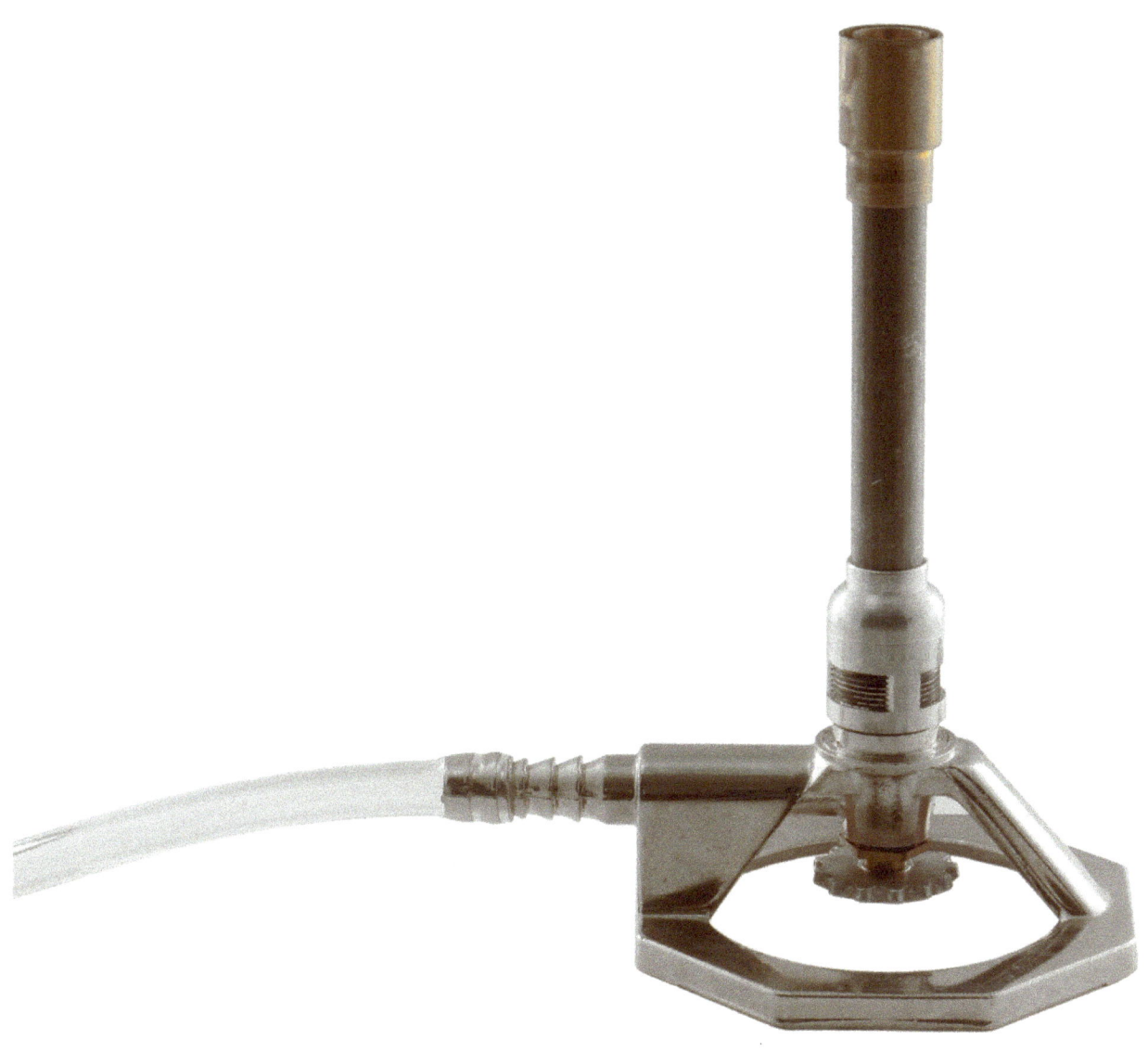

Bunsen Burner

ADN

DNA

Matraz Erlenmeyer (matraz cónico)

Erlenmeyer Flask (Conical Flask)

Cámara de goteo intravenosa

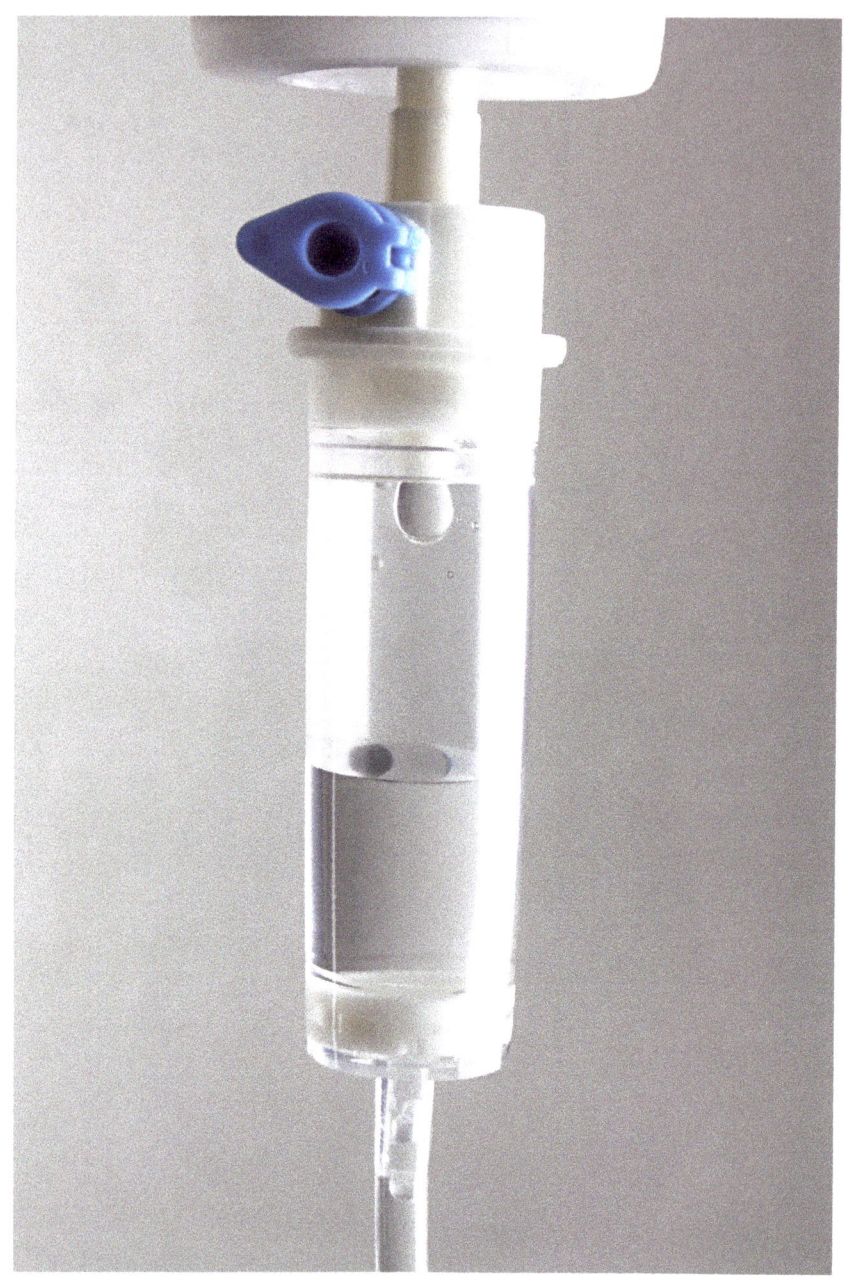

Intravenous Drip Chamber

Cristaleria de laboratorio

Lab Glassware

Microscopio professional de laboratorio

Professional Laboratory Microscope

Rata de laboratorio

Lab Rat

Laboratorio

Laboratory

Imán

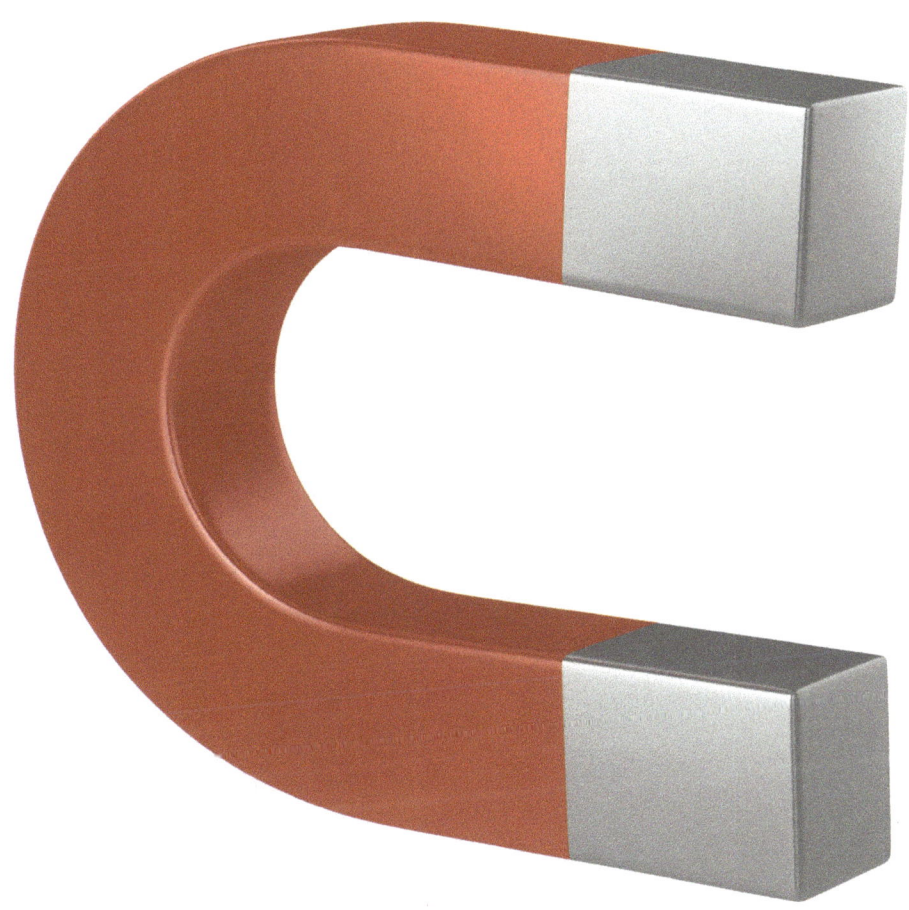

Magnet

Microscopio

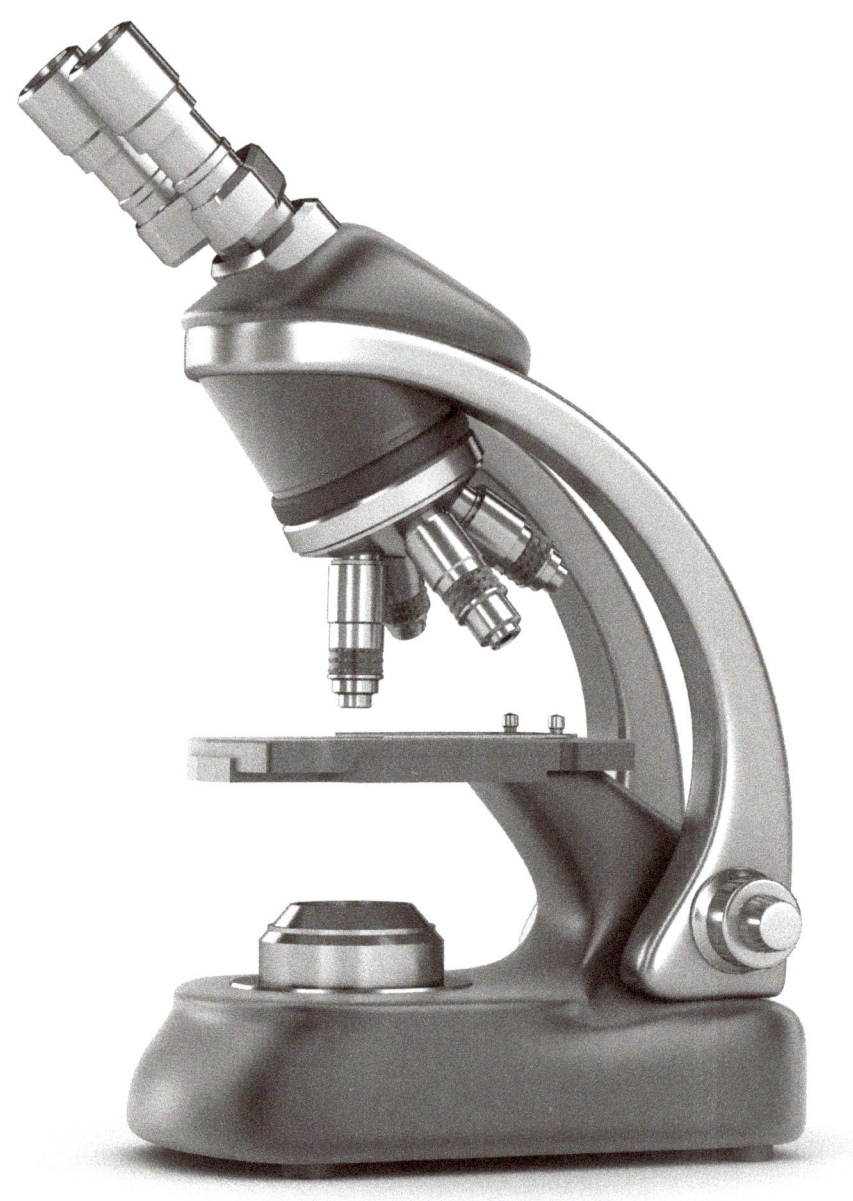

Microscope

Molécula

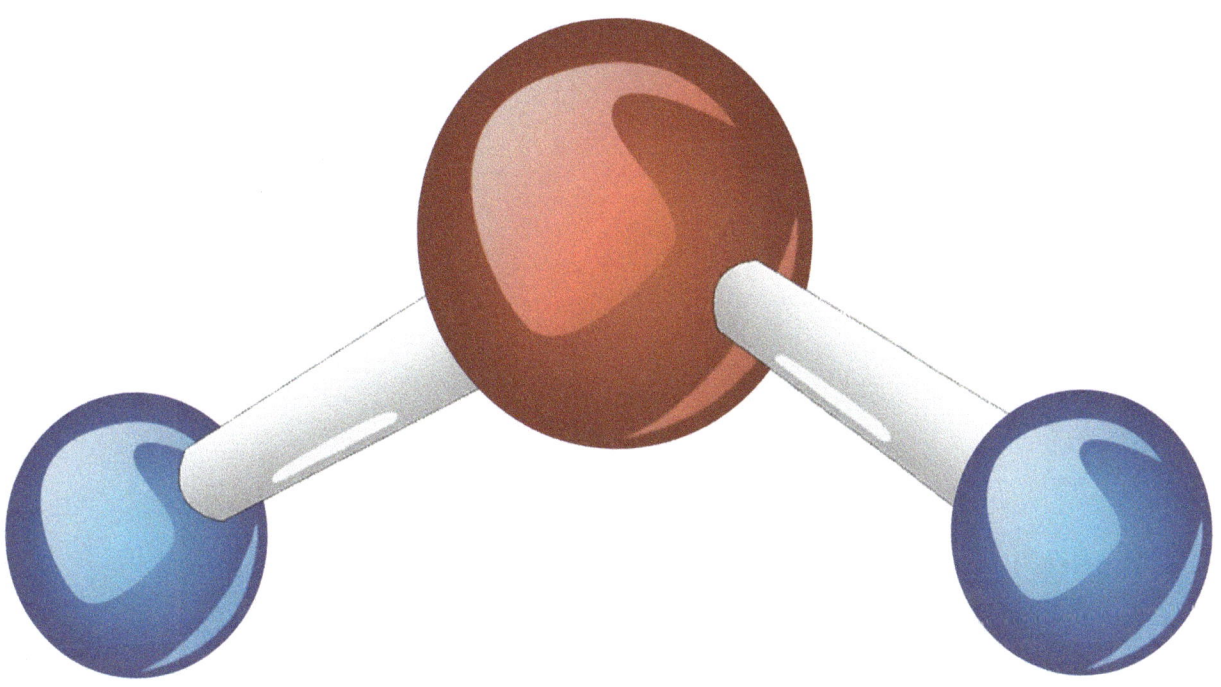

Molecule

Tabla periódica de elementos

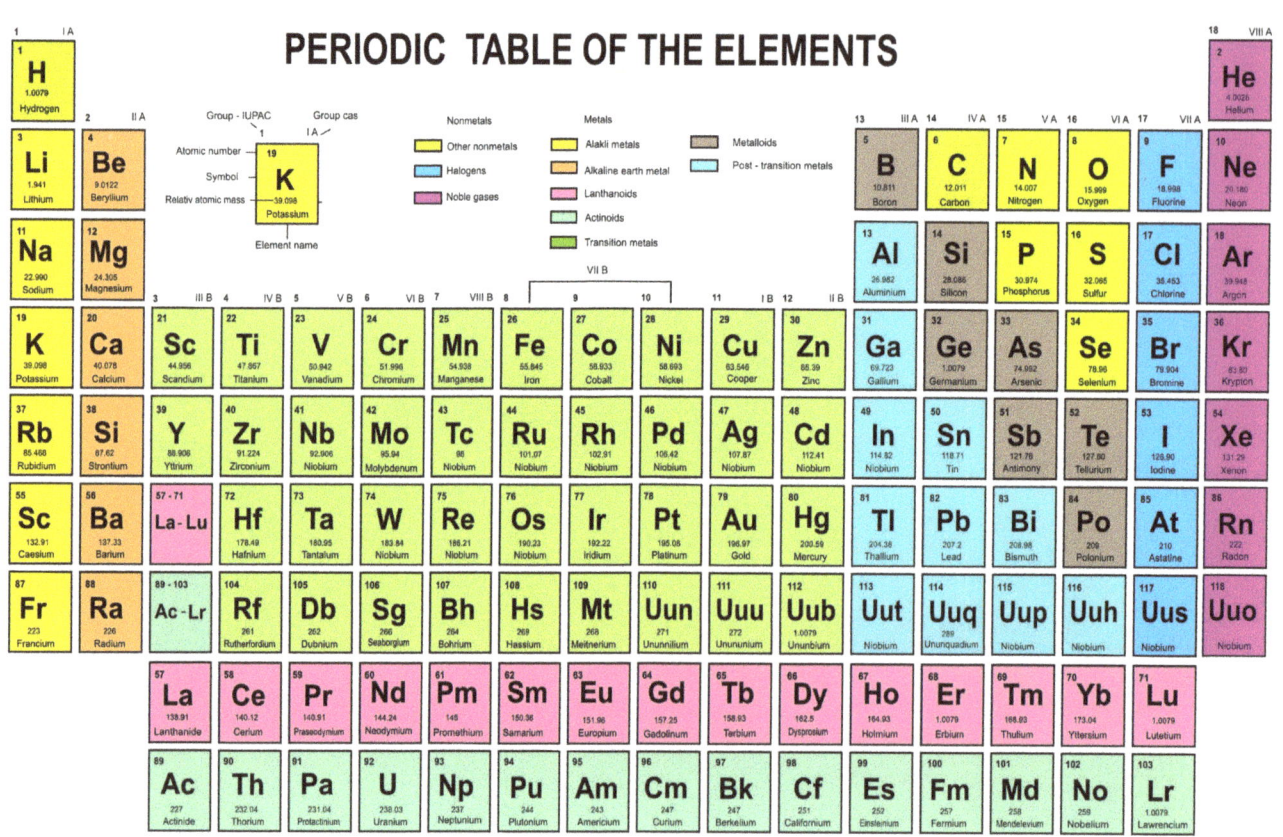

Periodic Table of the Elements

Plato de petri

Petri Dish

Robot

Robot

Gafas de seguridad

Safety Goggles

Científico

Scientist

Guantes estériles

Sterile Gloves

Tubos quirúrgicos

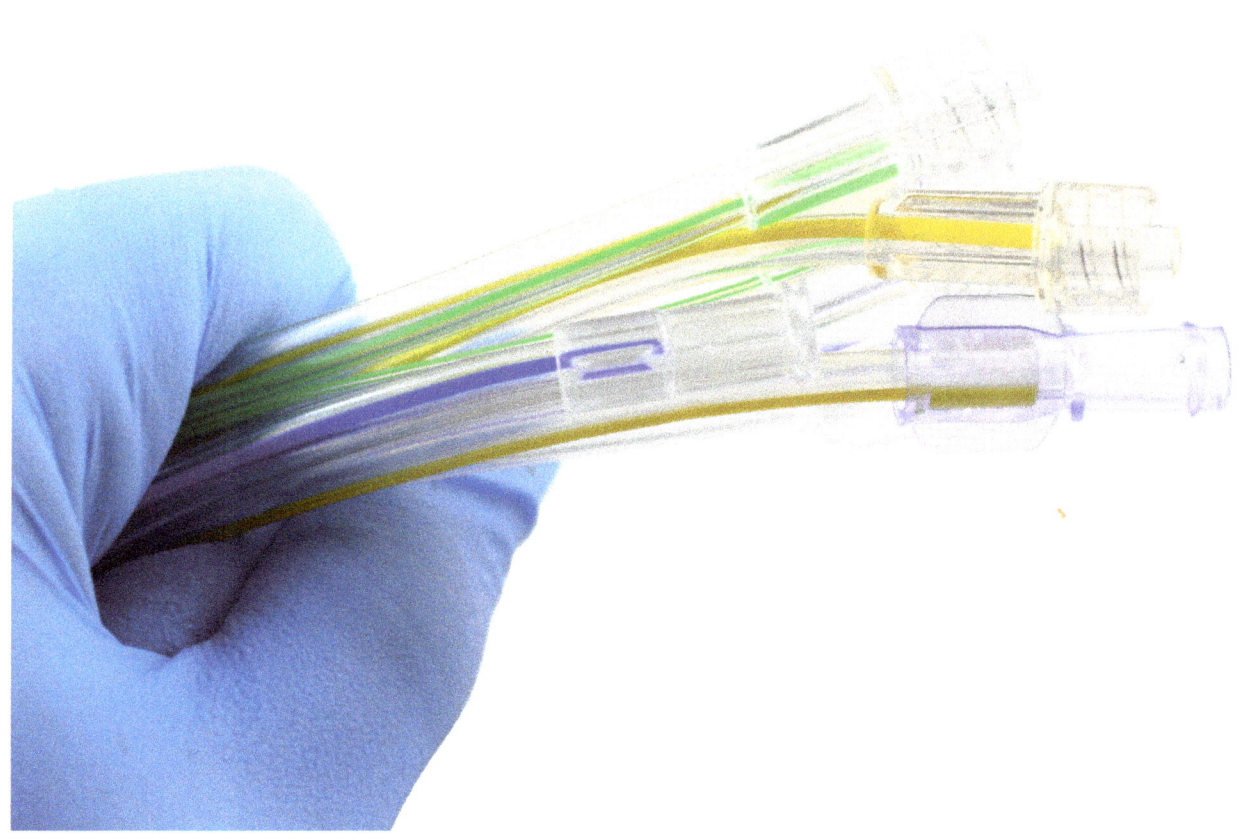

Surgical Tubing

Jeringa y viales

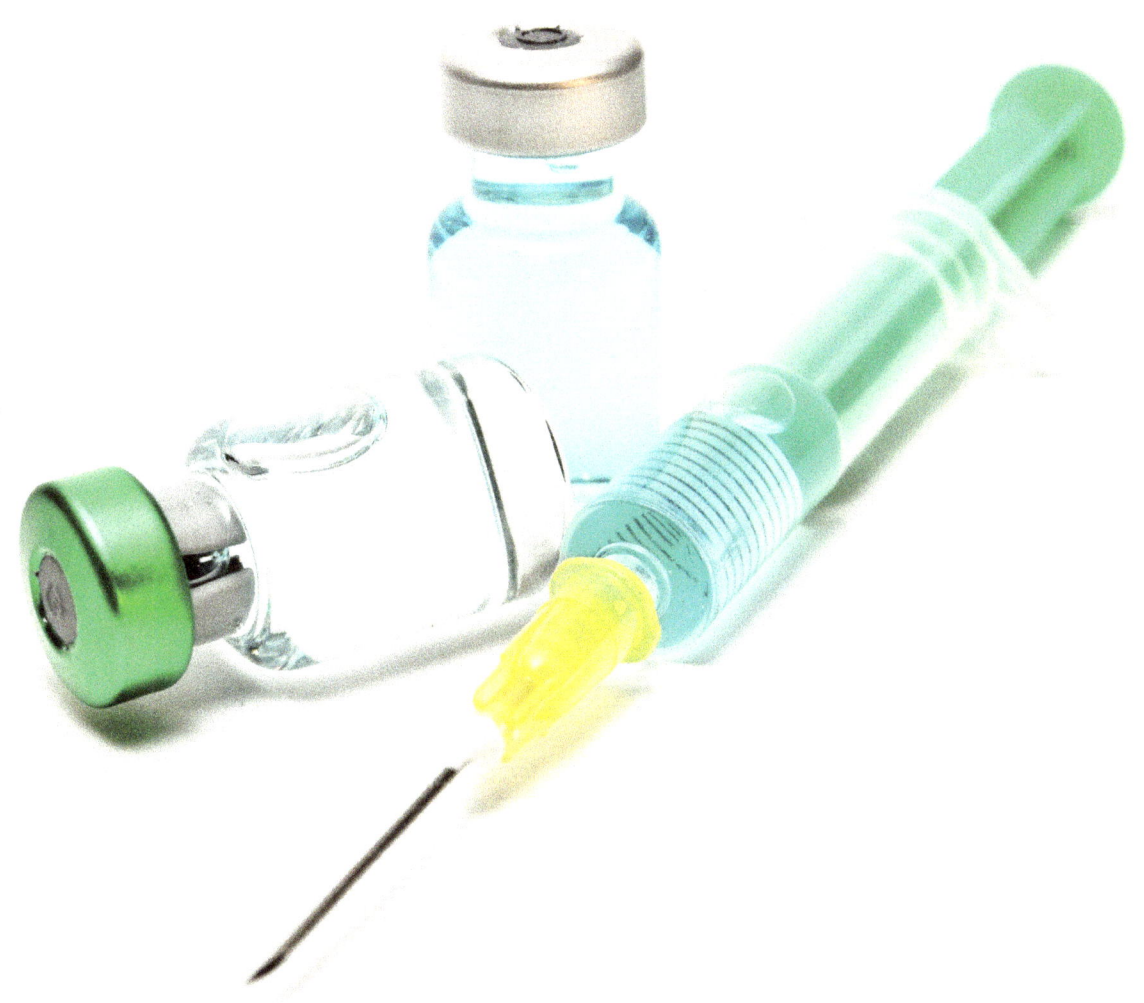

Syringe and Vials

Equipo de científicos

Team of Scientists

Viales

Vials

Make Sure to Check Out the Other Discover Series Books from Xist Publishing:

Published in the United States by Xist Publishing
www.xistpublishing.com
PO Box 61593 Irvine, CA 92602

© 2018 by Xist Publishing All rights reserved
Translated by Lenny Sandoval
No portion of this book may be reproduced without express permission of the publisher
All images licensed from Fotolia
First Bilingual Edition

ISBN: 978-1-5324-0772-7   eISBN: 978-1-5324-0773-4

xist Publishing

www.ingramcontent.com/pod-product-compliance
Lightning Source LLC
LaVergne TN
LVHW070950070426
835507LV00030B/3483